INSPIRING OTHERS

WORDS BY
STACY C. BAUER

ILLUSTRATIONS BY
EMANUELA NTAMACK

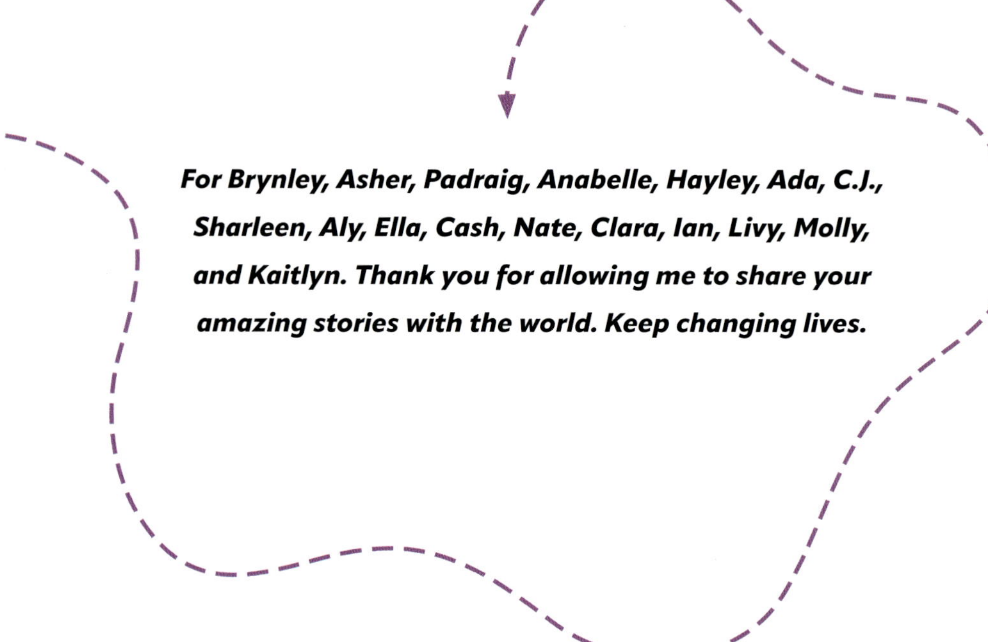

Cover and internal design by Travis Hasenour/Sourcebooks

Published by Sourcebooks eXplore, an imprint of Sourcebooks Kids
P.O. Box 4410, Naperville, Illinois 60567-4410
(630) 961-3900
sourcebookskids.com

Originally published in 2021 by Hop Off the Press, LLC

Cataloging-in-Publication Data is on file with the Library of Congress.

Source of Production: Chang Jiang Printing Media, Co., Chai Wan, Hong Kong, China
Date of Production: November 2024
Run Number: 5043203

Printed and bound in China.
CJ 10 9 8 7 6 5 4 3 2 1

MEET THE CHANGEMAKERS!

ANIMAL AMBASSADORS

These changemakers help advocate for animals.

CONSERVATION CREW

These changemakers are saving the planet.

INSPIRATIONAL ICONS

These changemakers are chasing their dreams and encouraging others to do the same.

HELPING HANDS

These changemakers are delivering support to those in need.

BRYNLEY
Oklahoma, USA
HELPING HANDS
"EVERYONE DESERVES TO BE HAPPY."
Merry Chri

DID YOU KNOW that being kind to others releases chemicals in our brains that make us feel happy and put us in a good mood? One single act of kindness is good for you, but in order to make the effects last, you need to make acts of kindness a regular practice, which is exactly what Brynley Meade does.

For Brynley's fifth birthday, she chose to donate toys to a local hospital instead of getting gifts for herself. Her mother put a note in her party invitations and posted her idea on social media. Family and friends responded generously. Brynley was excited to donate the gifts to the children at the hospital.

A crisis nursery is a place where families who are having an emergency can take their children for short-term care.

For her sixth birthday, Brynley wanted to do it again, but this time she wanted to let children in need choose their own toys. Her mother called the local crisis nursery and arranged for Brynley to donate toys. She personally gave a toy to every child there.

BRYNLEY'S FUN FACTS:

- Her favorite food is chicken with gravy.
- She loves to play Uno.
- Brynley's favorite colors are purple, pink, and turquoise.
- Her favorite animals are bunnies.

Then when she turned seven, Brynley decided to donate Christmas trees to nursing homes. Because of COVID, most nursing homes were locked down and the residents were lonely. Brynley wanted to make sure everyone had Christmas decorations to cheer them up. COVID prevented Brynley from having a birthday party, but through the power of social media, Amazon wish lists, and the help of her family and friends, Brynley reached her goal of eighty trees, one for each resident in a local long-term care center.

Brynley plans to continue helping people and spreading kindness in the future.

An **act of kindness** can make the other person feel important or recognized, especially at a time when they might be feeling sad or lonely.

BECOME A YOUNG CHANGEMAKERS HELPING HAND!

- Smile at someone every day.
- Try to notice when someone needs help, and help without being asked.
- Ask an adult to help you check out this website for more ideas: kindness.org.

BRYNLEY'S ADVICE FOR YOU:

Everyone can be a helper. Always be kind.

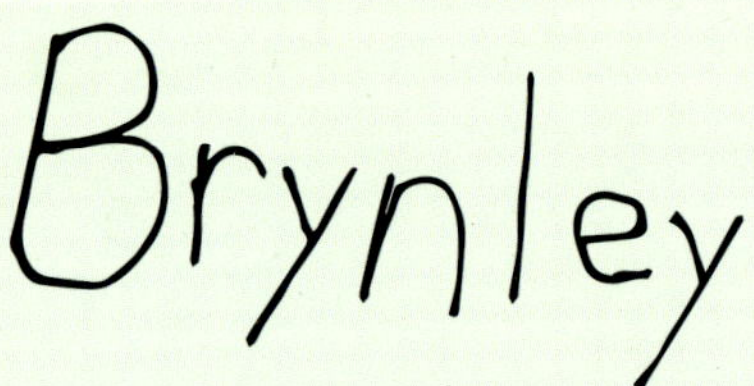

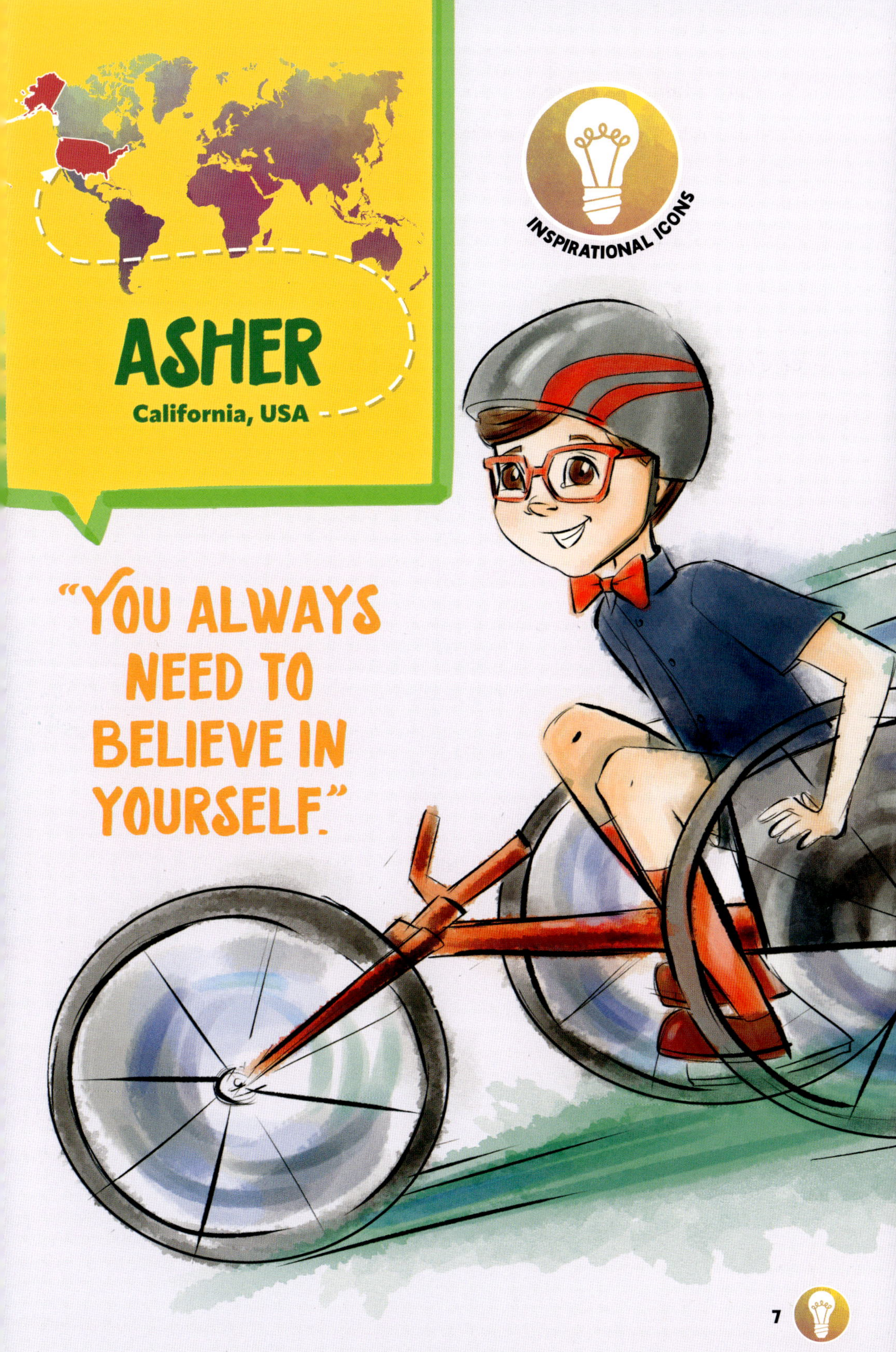
INSPIRATIONAL ICONS
ASHER
California, USA
"YOU ALWAYS NEED TO BELIEVE IN YOURSELF."

DO YOU HAVE a favorite sport? Have you ever dreamt of being in the Olympics? That is Asher's goal.

Asher Loera was born with spina bifida, which means his spine and spinal cord didn't form properly. He wears braces to walk but uses a wheelchair to travel longer distances.

When Asher was eighteen months old, his mother saw a flyer about a disability sports festival in their area. She brought Asher there, and he had the opportunity to try many different sports. At the festival his mother met Clayton Frech, the founder of **Angel City Sports**, and his son Ezra, an amputee who made the U.S. **Paralympic** team for high jump. Ezra became a huge inspiration for Asher. At the age of five, Asher competed in his first **adaptive sports** competition with Angel City Sports. It was then that he met his coach, Paralympian and gold medal winner Candace Cable. She saw his determination and focus and was excited to work with him. Asher has since tried many sports including basketball, swimming, shot put, javelin, golf, and tennis. He is classified as a seated athlete (competing from his wheelchair), which means he can't compete any other way and does not do any jumping sports. Of the sports he's tried, his favorites are wheelchair racing, wheelchair tennis, and golf.

ASHER'S FUN FACTS:

- He plays golf at least three times a week.
- He loves to sing and perform with his sisters.
- Asher loves to dance.

Having people in his life who have achieved lofty sports goals

Adaptive sports: Competitive or recreational sports for people with disabilities

Angel City Sports: An organization that provides free year-round adaptive sports opportunities for kids, adults, and veterans with physical disabilities or visual impairments

Paralympics: A series of international contests for athletes with disabilities that are held following the summer and winter Olympic Games

has pushed Asher to be his very best. In turn, Asher encourages younger athletes. He cheers on the other athletes he plays with, even his own competitors. Asher also encourages people to see that just because he has different abilities does not mean he can't play the same sports as everyone else. He has spoken at his school and in his classroom about his love of adaptive sports.

Being involved in the adaptive sports community and seeing athletes compete has given Asher strength and hope. Now, he hopes he can encourage other kids to go for their dreams, too.

BECOME A YOUNG CHANGEMAKERS INSPIRATIONAL ICON!

- Don't be afraid to push yourself out of your comfort zone and try new things!
- Go after your dreams—don't give up!

ASHER'S ADVICE FOR YOU:

Be confident, be brave, and believe in yourself.

"LET'S DO THIS!"

HELPING HANDS

DID YOU KNOW that around the world, about 690 million people go to bed hungry every night? Many people can't afford to eat nutritious food on a daily basis. Maybe you've experienced not knowing where your next meal is coming from or know someone who has.

You may not think you can do anything to help fill people's bellies, but Padraig Baron wants to tell you that you can! When Padraig was just two years old, he watched his mother help feed homeless people in Detroit. Right then and there, he decided he wanted to help, too! He took a small but very important step and asked his mom to buy granola bars to keep in the car. He wanted to hand them out himself to people through the car window.

That was just the beginning. Helping others became a way of life for Padraig. In 2020, during the COVID-19 pandemic, Padraig and his mother's nonprofit organization **Frugal On The Fly** signed up to distribute food boxes from the USDA's Farmers to Families program. They passed the food out to neighbors in need at a local plaza parking lot. They began with

PADRAIG'S FUN FACTS:

- Padraig enjoys hockey.
- He loves ice-cream cones with sprinkles.
- He likes science.

twenty-five families but quickly ran out of food. Padraig encouraged his mother to pick up more food to pass out.

Their Frugal On The Fly "Free Food Fridays" quickly grew, and soon they were giving 250 families free produce each week. They saw firsthand how the pandemic was affecting families. Some people found themselves in a food line for the very first time in their lives.

Padraig inspired his friends and family to jump in as volunteers. This resulted in a volunteer team of about forty people who served anywhere between 1,500 and 3,500 families weekly. The team ended up passing out one million pounds of fresh, nutritious food in twenty-three weeks!

Padraig's community outreach didn't stop there. He donated his books to Little Free Libraries in his neighborhood. With public libraries closed, he wanted to make sure kids had access to new books.

Padraig gathered used coats and hats from family and neighbors and helped a local coat drive get warm winter gear to people in need.

Helping out people in his community is important to Padraig; it makes his heart happy. Padraig dreams of being president one day. He wants to make the world a better place for everyone!

BECOME A YOUNG CHANGEMAKERS HELPING HAND!

- Visit frugalonthefly.com to learn more about Padraig's mission.
- Visit foodrescue.us to read more about food rescue in the United States.
- Go through your clothes, books, and toys. Choose some to donate to a local shelter.

PADRAIG'S ADVICE FOR YOU:

If you can't find organizations allowing kid volunteers, start your own projects. You can do something by yourself and still make a difference. Then, get your friends involved. One person can make a difference.

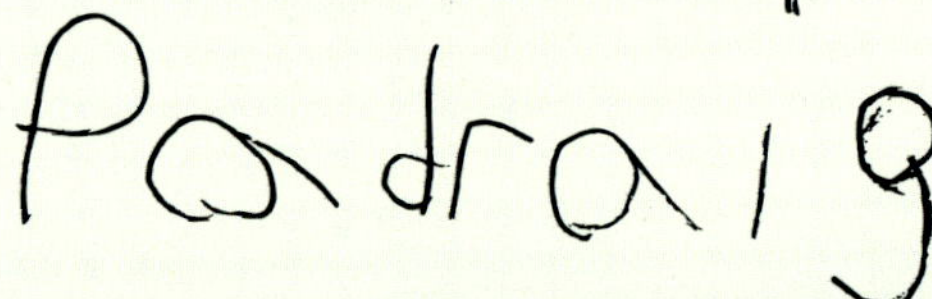

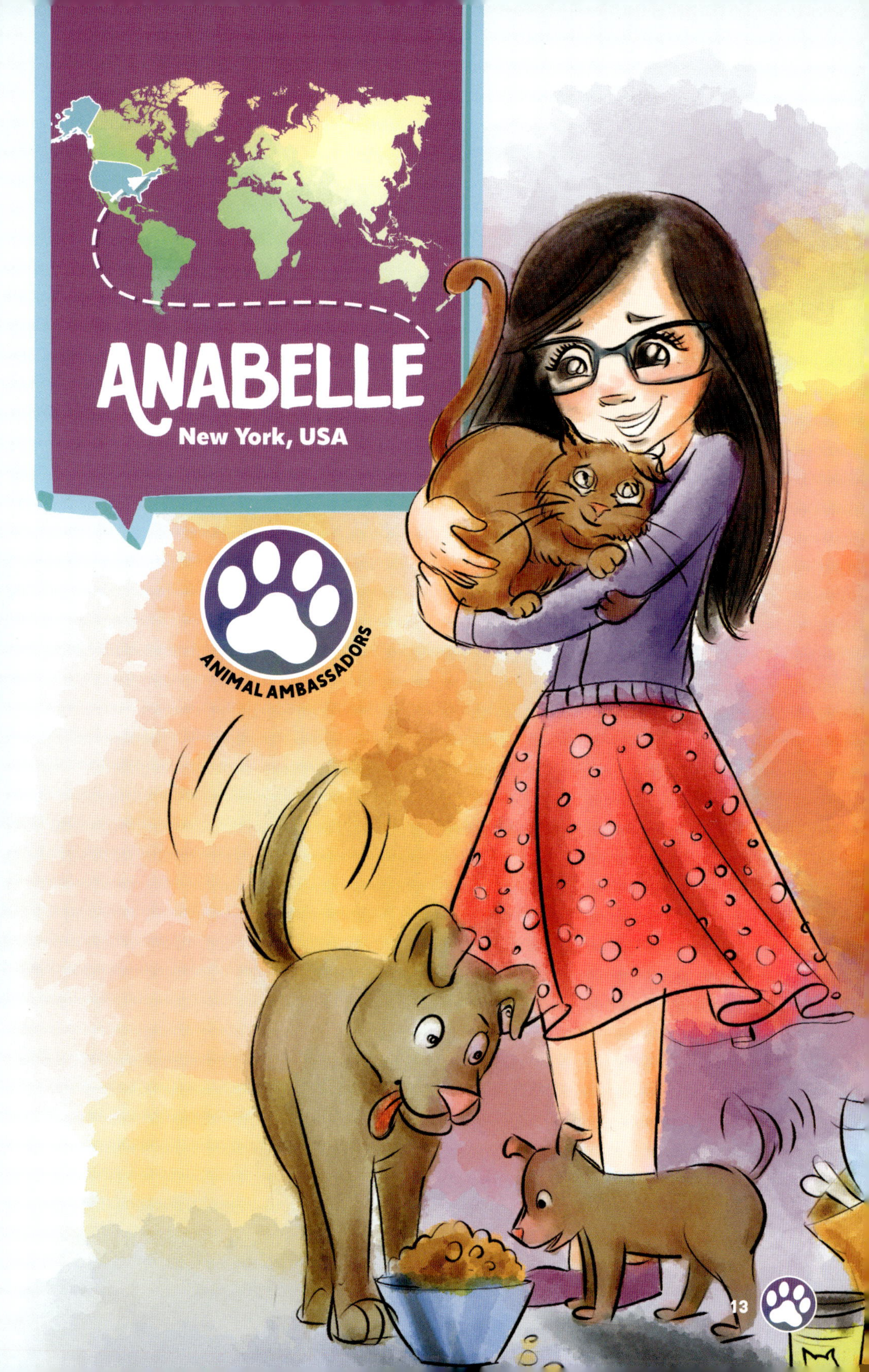
ANABELLE
New York, USA
ANIMAL AMBASSADORS

"HELPING ANIMALS IS THE BEST GIFT OF ALL."

ANABELLE ABRAMS HAS always had a soft spot in her heart for animals. One Christmas, when she was seven years old, Anabelle was feeling sad for all of the animals who were alone over the holidays. That inspired her to take action.

Since Anabelle's birthday is December 18, she and her mom decided to put a note inside of her birthday invitations asking for pet supplies to be donated instead of birthday gifts. Anabelle was amazed and overwhelmed by the response and generosity of her family and friends. She delivered all of the supplies to a local animal shelter that helps place abandoned or orphaned animals into their forever homes. For Anabelle, one of the most enjoyable parts of the donation was putting all of the supplies under the shelter's Christmas tree.

Anabelle has since turned this into an annual tradition. Every year on her birthday, Anabelle collects donations instead of gifts, then drops the supplies off at the shelter. She loves knowing that the animals will get Christmas presents, too. And of course she loves the chance to hold and cuddle the animals! Anabelle plans to continue her yearly tradition and hopes to collect more supplies each year. She also had the idea to host a "LemonARF" stand to sell lemonade and donate the proceeds to the animal shelter. When she's older, Anabelle wants to volunteer at the shelter and foster kittens.

ANABELLE'S FUN FACTS:

- Her family has a friendly deer named Tick Tick that visits their house.
- Her family fostered and adopted two kitties.
- She loves reading Percy Jackson and Greek mythology.

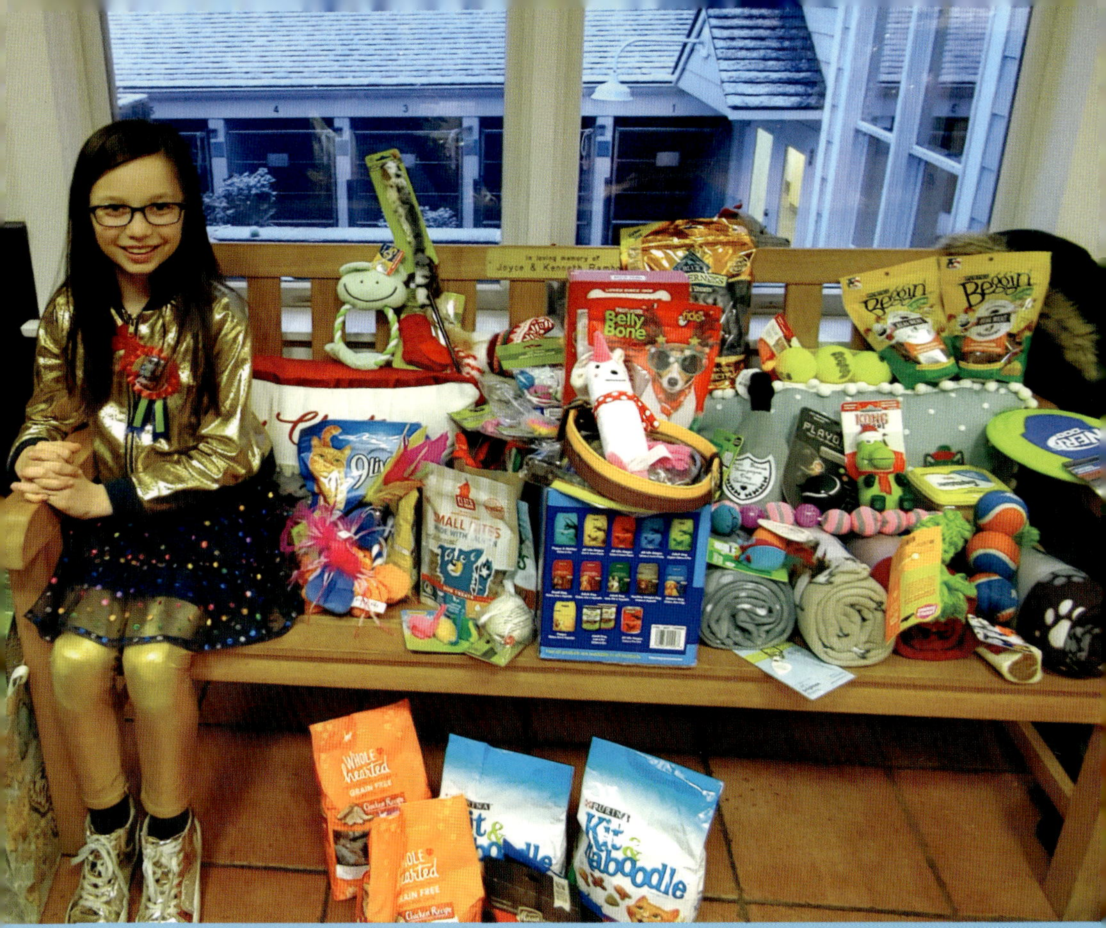

BECOME A YOUNG CHANGEMAKERS ANIMAL AMBASSADOR!

- Find an animal shelter in your area. Can you volunteer there? Do they need supplies? Find out what you can do to help!

ANABELLE'S ADVICE FOR YOU:

Making a difference is all about finding something that matters to you and your community and trying to make it better. If we all try, this world would be a better place.

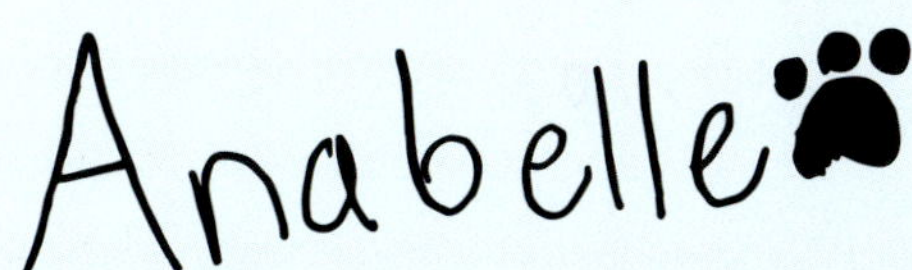

HAYLEY

Illinois, USA

HELPING HANDS

"STAY KIND!"

MOST PEOPLE THINK you need to be an adult in order to make a difference in the world and that you need to do something huge or spend a lot of money. People are wrong—there are young people who are taking small steps to solve problems every day! Hayley Orlinsky is one of them.

When Hayley was just seven years old and heard that hospitals were running out of masks and other **PPE** during the early stages of the **COVID-19 pandemic**, she was inspired to use her love of making friendship bracelets to help. Hayley decided to try to sell **Rainbow Loom** bracelets and donate the money to her local hospital.

The first thing she did was

Personal protective equipment (PPE) is specialized clothing or equipment worn to protect people against disease. It can include masks, gowns, and gloves.

COVID-19 is a disease that was first seen at the end of 2019. It can cause mild to severe respiratory illness.

Rainbow Loom bracelets are made by weaving tiny elastic bands together.

create a price list and samples of the bracelets. Hayley then created a video about her mission, showing the different samples and prices. Her mom posted it on social media. With friends, family, and even strangers buying bracelets, it only took a few hours for her to fly past her original goal of $200! She set a new goal of $10,000. When she reached that, she pushed for another $10,000 and another. Her ultimate ending point was $50,000, which she never thought she'd meet. In her mind, she would be making a few hundred bracelets, but her mission grew so huge that it took over her entire house! Hayley's project went on for fourteen months—that's when she reached her $50,000 goal.

Hayley could not have done this on her own. She taught friends and family how to make bracelets so they could help her fulfill orders. She created a video tutorial which they sent to people and even taught people how to make the bracelets live over Zoom! She received gift cards from craft stores, such as Michaels and JOANN Fabrics, to help pay for rubber bands. People donated funds and supplies. Four hundred kids and counselors at Hayley's summer camp also made bracelets. She came home with hundreds of bracelets every day! Hayley was inspired by everyone who stepped up to help her. Some celebrities even got involved in her cause! Drew Barrymore and Carrie Underwood each donated and Drew even featured Hayley on her talk show! After word of mouth spread, the organizers of the Grammy Awards chose to feature her bracelets in the official swag bags at the ceremony!

The money Hayley's team raised for the hospital helped provide masks and PPE to low-income families too! Even though it was hard work, Hayley never lost sight of why she was doing it. She followed her dreams and changed lives!

BECOME A YOUNG CHANGEMAKERS HELPING HAND!

- Do you enjoy making crafts or art? You could sell your art and donate the funds to a cause you care about.
- Buy crafts or art made that will benefit a charity.

HAYLEY'S FUN FACTS:

- Hayley has been dancing since she was eighteen months old. She has done ballet, tap, hip-hop, jazz, funk, lyrical, contemporary, and acro.
- Hayley wants to be a news anchor when she grows up so she can report on positive and uplifting stories.
- She is the oldest of three sisters.

HAYLEY'S ADVICE FOR YOU:

Find something you love to do and see if there's a way to use it to help others.

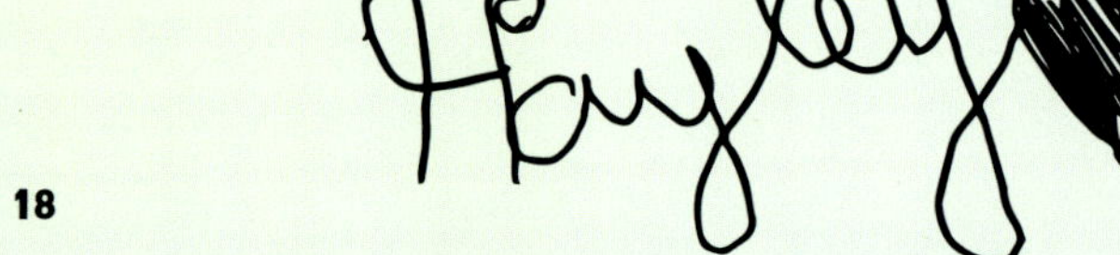

ADA

West Yorkshire, England

"I LOVE RUNNING AND RAISING PENNIES FOR CLDF."

ADA BUTTERFIELD WAS born with a rare, and often fatal, type of liver disease called biliary atresia, in which the **bile ducts** are clogged. Bile is a fluid made by the liver, an organ that gets rid of waste. Usually the bile travels from the liver to the small intestines, but in Ada's case, it was getting backed up, which damaged her liver.

At five weeks old, Ada had a lifesaving operation, and although it helped, she will need checkups and medication for the rest of her life. Ada may even need a new liver one day. When the Children's Liver Disease Foundation (CLDF) learned about Ada, they quickly stepped up to help her and her family and give them hope and support.

Since then, Ada has done her best to give back. When a marathon her mom was planning to run in April 2020 was cancelled because of the COVID-19 pandemic, Ada decided to create her own running event. Better yet, she used that opportunity to raise money for the charity that had given them so much support. Her family spread the word on social media and planned a route through Ada's neighborhood. Ada's friends lined the streets and cheered her on. She raised over

ADA'S FUN FACTS:

- Ada loves cabbage.
- Ada is a night owl—she loves staying up late.
- Her favorite people are her cousins, Eliza and Violet.

$5,000 for CLDF with this one event alone!

Through this fundraiser, Ada found her own love of running—and of giving back. Ada set a goal to run twenty miles over the course of a month. Her parents used social media to let people know that she would be doing this challenge, and people started donating in Ada's name. Inspired by Ada, over 230 other kids decided to join her in running for charity!

Ada and her parents have raised over $100,000 for the charity so far and have no plans to stop fundraising any time soon.

Bile ducts are tubes that carry bile, a fluid made by the liver that gets rid of waste, to the small intestines.

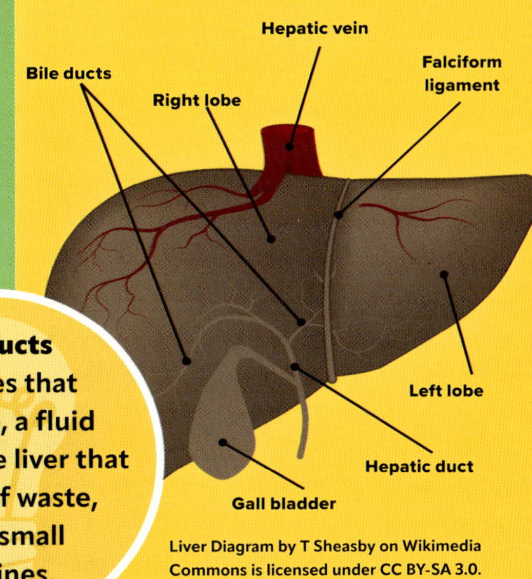

Liver Diagram by T Sheasby on Wikimedia Commons is licensed under CC BY-SA 3.0. Labels adjusted.

LET'S LEARN ABOUT THE LIVER!

Your liver is an organ with many important jobs including:

- Cleaning your blood.
- Producing an important digestive liquid called bile.
- Storing energy in the form of a sugar called glycogen.

BECOME A YOUNG CHANGEMAKERS INSPIRATIONAL ICON!

- Talk to an adult about donating to Ada's cause at childliverdisease.org.
- Brainstorm ways to raise money for charity.

ADA'S ADVICE FOR YOU:

Just do it, it makes you feel good and happy!

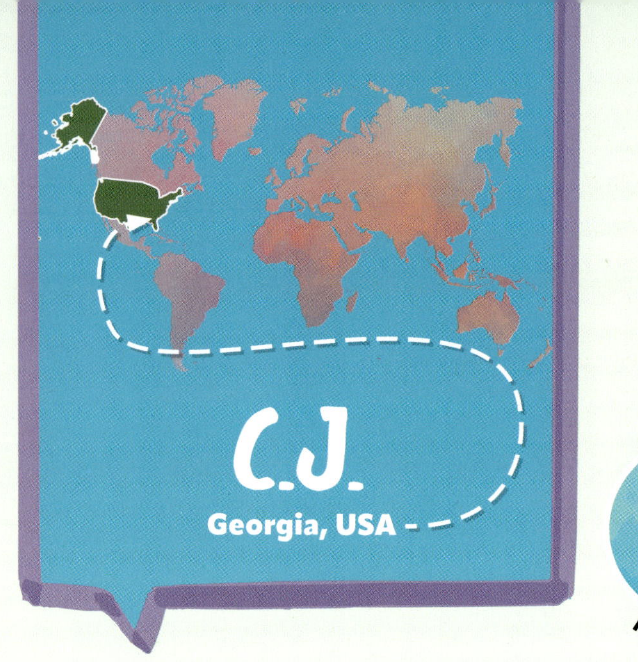

"THE BLANKETS I GIVE AREN'T MERELY PRESENTS, THEY ARE MORE ABOUT PRESENCE AND LETTING CHILDREN KNOW THAT SOMEONE CARES ABOUT THEM. I WAS ONCE A KID EXPERIENCING SOMETHING HARD—THE GRIEF OF LOSING A SIBLING—AND JUST HAVING THE SUPPORT OF MY FAMILY AND A COMFY BLANKET MADE ME FEEL SAFE."

AFTER LOSING HIS baby sister when he was just five years old, C.J. Matthews was inspired to do something to help other kids healing from traumatic situations. Since blankets have always been one of his favorite things, he decided to raise money to buy blankets and donate them to kids in need of comfort. C.J. and his family ran a GoFundMe campaign so family and friends across the country could contribute. They also teamed up with a friend to host a drop-off event at her place of business.

Local newspapers advertised the event, and people donated more than six hundred blankets! Many of the blankets donated were throw blankets, but members from a local moms' group donated crocheted and other handmade blankets. Those were used as a special donation to babies in the **NICU** in honor of C.J.'s baby sister.

As much as C.J. liked the idea of donating blankets, what he really wanted was to make sure the blankets got to the kids who needed them. He and his family contacted local hospitals, orphan relief centers, group homes, and different types of shelters (homeless, emergency, domestic violence, and those for teen moms).

C.J. and his family turned their collection event into an annual winter tradition and called it **Blankies 4 My Buddies**.

But C.J. didn't stop with donated blankets. He also helps kids make do-it-yourself (DIY) blankets through a program he started called **the Blanket Box Project** Participants receive a

NICU stands for newborn intensive care unit. This is a nursery in a hospital that provides around-the-clock care to sick or premature babies (babies born early).

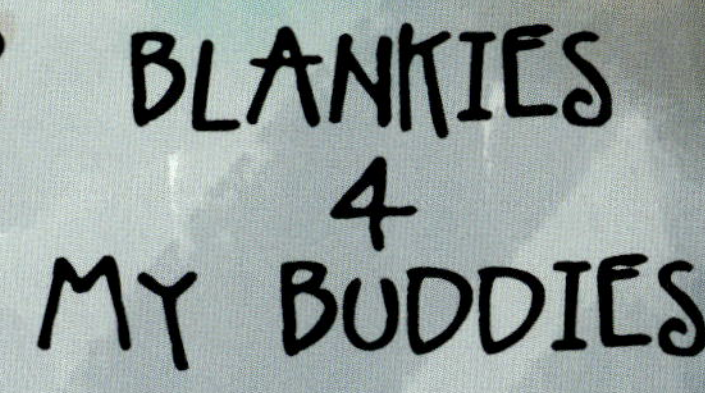

DIY blanket kit, with which they can make a special custom blanket to share with someone they know or even a stranger who is in need of comfort.

C.J.'s future plans include expanding his project to help even more people on a larger scale. He is developing his own line of blankets and other products! His ultimate goal is to create a social impact company that donates one blanket to a child in need for every blanket that is purchased. C.J. wants you to know that you're never too young or too old to use your voice to make a difference.

C.J.'S FUN FACTS:

- He is afraid of most bugs!
- Gumbo is his favorite food.
- C.J.'s dog Bentley is older than he is, and he has two turtles—one of which he's had since he was four years old.

BECOME A YOUNG CHANGEMAKERS HELPING HAND!

- Talk to your family about supporting underserved kids in your area.
- Be kind to people—you never know what someone else is going through.
- Visit C.J.'s website with an adult to see how you can help! blankies4mybuddies.org

C.J.'S ADVICE FOR YOU:

Just do it. It doesn't matter how big or small your idea is—any act of kindness matters and goes a long way. My mom always reminds me that people will forget what you say or do but will always remember how you made them feel. A genuine act of kindness from a friend or a stranger will always be remembered.

C.J.

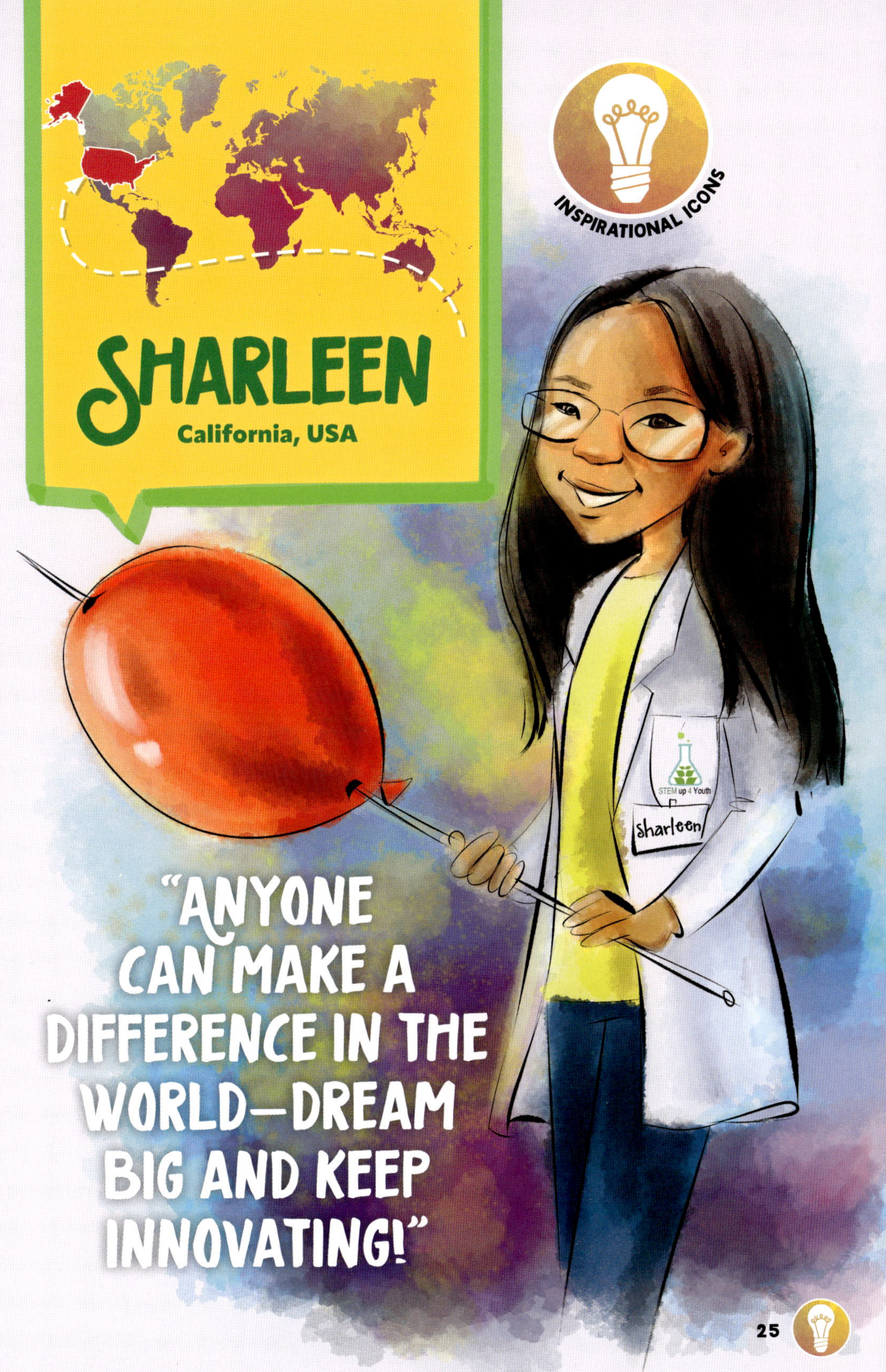
SHARLEEN
California, USA
INSPIRATIONAL ICONS
STEM up 4 Youth
Sharleen
"ANYONE CAN MAKE A DIFFERENCE IN THE WORLD—DREAM BIG AND KEEP INNOVATING!"

SHARLEEN LOH HAS been curious about the world around her since she was a young child. Her parents fueled her natural curiosity by bringing her to STEM fairs. STEM stands for Science, Technology, Engineering, and Mathematics. It helps explain how and why things work, how to invent things, and how to solve problems. For Sharleen, STEM fairs were love at first sight. She couldn't get enough of the experiments and was always asking questions about how and why the experiments turned out the way they did.

As she got older, she wondered why other kids her age didn't share the same love of STEM. She remembered all of the fun STEM activities she was exposed to as a child and decided to try to make STEM programs available to kids who didn't have access to them.

As she researched STEM, Sharleen learned that not only were the experiments cool, but STEM education improves creative thinking, encourages teamwork, and helps children develop communication. It also empowers critical thinking, improves social skills, and boosts curiosity—all important life skills.

When she was thirteen years old, Sharleen approached the principal and PTA (Parent Teacher Association) at her school, who agreed to let her host a STEM night. She spent nine months researching and planning the event,

SHARLEEN'S FUN FACTS:

- In kindergarten, her dream job was to be a "pizza lady!"
- Her favorite food is a dessert that her grandmother loved to make for her throughout childhood: 湯圓 (tāng yuan)—sweet, chewy rice balls served in soup.
- In her free time, she loves crocheting little stuffed animals (amigurumi) for her friends and family.

Underprivileged children don't have the advantages many other children have. They usually live in poverty.

which over seven hundred people attended. It was so successful and she got so much positive feedback that her principal turned it into an annual event!

A few weeks later, Sharleen initiated the first STEM program at a local club where **underprivileged** children went after school. She designed her STEM activities around hands-on experimentation, involvement, and fun! This allowed children to explore their natural curiosity. Eventually, attendance in her program grew and she had to recruit volunteers (whom she calls STEMbers) to help.

BECOME A YOUNG CHANGEMAKERS INSPIRATIONAL ICON!

- Get curious: What do you wonder about? Write some ideas down, then try to find the answers.
- Visit stemup4youth.com with the help of an adult for more information about Sharleen's program.
- Push yourself out of your comfort zone. Don't be afraid to try something new.

Sharleen turned her program into the nonprofit organization **STEMup4Youth** and started receiving invitations to host large STEM events. To keep up with the requests, she recruited more STEMbers and formed chapters of STEMup4Youth. Today, there are seventeen chapters and four divisions reaching 59,000 children around the world! Her goal is to continue to inspire children around the world to be excited about and pursue STEM.

SHARLEEN'S ADVICE FOR YOU:

Anyone can make a difference in the world—dream big and keep innovating!

HOSPITAL
ALY
Pennsylvania, USA
HELPING HANDS
"CHANGING THE WORLD, ONE MONKEY AT A TIME."

IS THERE SOMETHING special that makes you feel better when you're sick? Maybe it's a person, a pet, a book, a special meal, or a toy. For Aly, it was a stuffed monkey.

When Alyson Creasy was eight years old, she was hospitalized with an illness. While in the emergency room, her grandmother gave her a stuffed monkey to comfort her. Having something to hold onto did make Aly feel better, and she was inspired to help other children in the same way.

Aly decided that since it was a stuffed monkey that comforted her, she would give stuffed monkeys to other kids in the hospital. She sat down with her family to figure out how to achieve her goal. She created a spreadsheet with goals of how many monkeys she wanted to be able to donate. Then, she started to share her vision with people. Aly's community came together and helped her raise money. She began with simple "monkey drops" at area hospitals but slowly began to grow those monkey drops. Around the same time, Aly received a note from a family who had read about her movement. Their young daughter, Olivia, had passed away, and they were looking for a charity to support in her memory. Aly knew at once what to do.

She worked with a local company to create a unique monkey she could donate, and she named it the "Olivia Monkey." Now, **Aly's Monkey Movement** has sent out over seven thousand monkeys!!

Aly's Monkey Movement has expanded to provide a more personal service, too—it gives people the opportunity to personally request monkeys for specific people. Aly and her siblings tag and name each monkey according to the sponsor's name or request before they are sent to their forever homes. The tag invites the recipient and their monkey to share a photo on Aly's Facebook page. This gives the community the opportunity to meet the children they sponsor.

Aly's movement is growing by the day and is full of positive supporters who rally around these families with love, encouragement, and guidance. Together Aly hopes they can change the world, one monkey at a time.

BECOME A YOUNG CHANGEMAKERS HELPING HAND!

- Do something kind for children in a hospital near you. Make cards or colorful posters.
- Visit alysmonkeys.org with the help of an adult to find out how to request a monkey for someone in need.
- Talk to your family or friends about donating toward Aly's cause!

ALY'S FUN FACTS:

- She's afraid of spiders!
- Aly loves basketball.
- She loves doing magic tricks.

ALY'S ADVICE FOR YOU:

Be a leader, not a follower—unless you're following your heart!

Aly

ELLA AND CASH

Florida, USA, and Tennessee, USA

"THE YOUTHS OF TODAY ARE THE ADULTS OF TOMORROW!"

—ELLA

"KIDS MAY BE A SMALL PART OF THE POPULATION, BUT WE ARE 100 PERCENT OF THE FUTURE, AND WE CAN CHANGE THE WORLD."

—CASH

CONSERVATION CREW

DID YOU KNOW that 80 percent of ocean trash comes from waterways that drain into them? Ella Grace and Cash Daniels were both worried about the amount of garbage, especially plastic, that ends up in the ocean and the effect it has on animals and the environment. They learned about the problem at the young age of five years old and started doing research and learning more. When they were seven, they took action.

Even though they hadn't met yet, they both began by doing cleanups. Cash started by cleaning up rivers. He organized the cleanups with family and friends and adopted a mile of the

Tennessee River. Cash goes out every week, sometimes more, to clean up the river—unfortunately, there is always more trash! Ella also started organizing family, friend, and neighborhood cleanups at the age of seven. She began by focusing on cleaning up Lake Ontario when she lived in Canada. Then, when she moved to Florida, she began focusing on the ocean.

In June 2019, they both attended the **Ocean Heroes Boot Camp** in Vancouver, Canada. That's where they met and learned that they were passionate about many of the same things. Ella and Cash became fast friends as they talked for hours about all of their big dreams for the environment. They decided that they could make an even bigger difference in the world if they worked together, so they started a nonprofit, **The Cleanup Kids**, to help encourage kids around the world to use their voices and their actions to help clean up the environment. Kids can become Cleanup Kids by filling out a form on their website and pledging to do at least one cleanup per month. During the cleanups they're encouraged to take photos, count how many pieces of garbage were picked up, and dispose of the trash correctly. One of their big initiatives is the **One Million Piece Pickup**, when they set a goal to pick up a million pieces of trash globally in one year!

Ella and Cash plan on continuing their efforts to help the environment. They have been featured on the news, given presentations about plastic pollution, and spoken to government leaders about what they think needs to happen to protect our earth and its animals.

Ella and Cash have been told that they are too young to be doing these things and that their voices don't matter. They want to tell you that that's not true! Ella was a part of two bills that were written to protect ocean animals in Canada. Cash has picked up fifteen thousand pounds from the Tennessee River alone! Combined, they have picked up over twenty-five thousand pounds

The **Ocean Heroes Boot Camp** empowers youth to take action against ocean plastic pollution.

of garbage. They have both inspired other people to clean up trash too. It doesn't matter how old you are—you CAN make a difference in the world!

BECOME A YOUNG CHANGEMAKERS CONSERVATION CREW MEMBER!

- Ask an adult to help you visit thecleanupkids.org to learn more about Ella and Cash's nonprofit.
- Give up plastic straws, plastic bags, and single-use water bottles.

ELLA'S FUN FACTS:

- Ella likes to scuba dive.
- She loves to read.
- She enjoys playing *Minecraft*.

CASH'S FUN FACTS:

- Cash loves visiting national parks.
- His favorite animal is the whale shark.
- His favorite river is the Tennessee River, which is actually the most polluted with microplastics in the world!

ELLA'S ADVICE FOR YOU:

If you have an idea you think might make a change, then do it. My mom and dad tell me that we learn a lot from things that didn't work out how we wanted them. So just keep learning and one day you will make something amazing that can save the ocean or corals or maybe protect an endangered species. Keep trying.

CASH'S ADVICE FOR YOU:

There are a lot of things everybody can do. Be brave when talking to people, because your opinion matters just as much as theirs does.

Ella Cash

"MISSIONS HELP PEOPLE WHO RELY MOSTLY ON YOU TO HELP THEM GET THROUGH THE YEAR. PLAY WITH CHICKENS SECOND, DO THE WORK FIRST!"

HELPING HANDS

HAVE YOU EVER gone on a mission trip, or do you know someone who has? Ian, Nate, Clara, and Livy McNair wanted to help people living in Haiti, a very poor island nation in the Caribbean, which has suffered from many hurricanes.

Because their church supports an orphanage there, the family was given an opportunity to go on a mission trip—a trip where people spend time helping those in need.

Although only older brothers Ian and Nate were able to go on the trip with their father, Clara and Livy helped, too, by drawing pictures and selling them to collect money for the people of Haiti.

When they arrived, the boys were shocked to find that the orphanage did not have electricity, indoor plumbing, or air-conditioning. With so little space, the orphans slept in beds stacked on top of each other. There were between six and eight kids per room, with separate buildings for the boys and girls. They were also surprised to find that the kids didn't have toys, which meant the children had to create fun out of whatever they could find—including chickens!

Ian and Nate knew they couldn't solve all of the orphanage's problems, but they wanted to do what they could. They helped repair the school and medical buildings at the orphanage and helped their dad build a water collection gutter system, since the Haitians don't have clean drinking water.

Seeing how other people live made Ian and Nate more grateful for what they have. It upset them to see that not all kids have a good life. They want to go back someday to help again, especially Nate, who wants to be a doctor one day. He would like to see how their hospitals work without modern equipment to better understand how he can help. Clara and Livy hope to go when they are old enough.

Haiti is in the western third of the island of Hispaniola between the Caribbean Sea and the North Atlantic Ocean. Haiti is the poorest country in the Latin American and Caribbean regions and is among the poorest countries in the world.

BECOME A YOUNG CHANGEMAKERS HELPING HAND!

- Raise money for a charity that you love: Set up lemonade stands. Have a bake sale. Have a car wash with your friends.
- Look for ways to volunteer in your community.
- Look into taking a mission trip with your family.

THE McNAIR KIDS' FUN FACTS:

- Livy likes dance, art, and gymnastics. She was adopted from the Congo.
- Ian loves soccer and enjoyed playing it with the Haitian children, who love it as well.
- Nate plans to be a doctor and wants to study infectious disease.
- Clara hopes to grow up and train service dogs. She enjoys making slime and dog treats.

THEIR ADVICE FOR YOU:

You don't have to travel overseas to make a difference. You can find a local charity to support right in your own community.

Livy Nate Ian Clara ♡

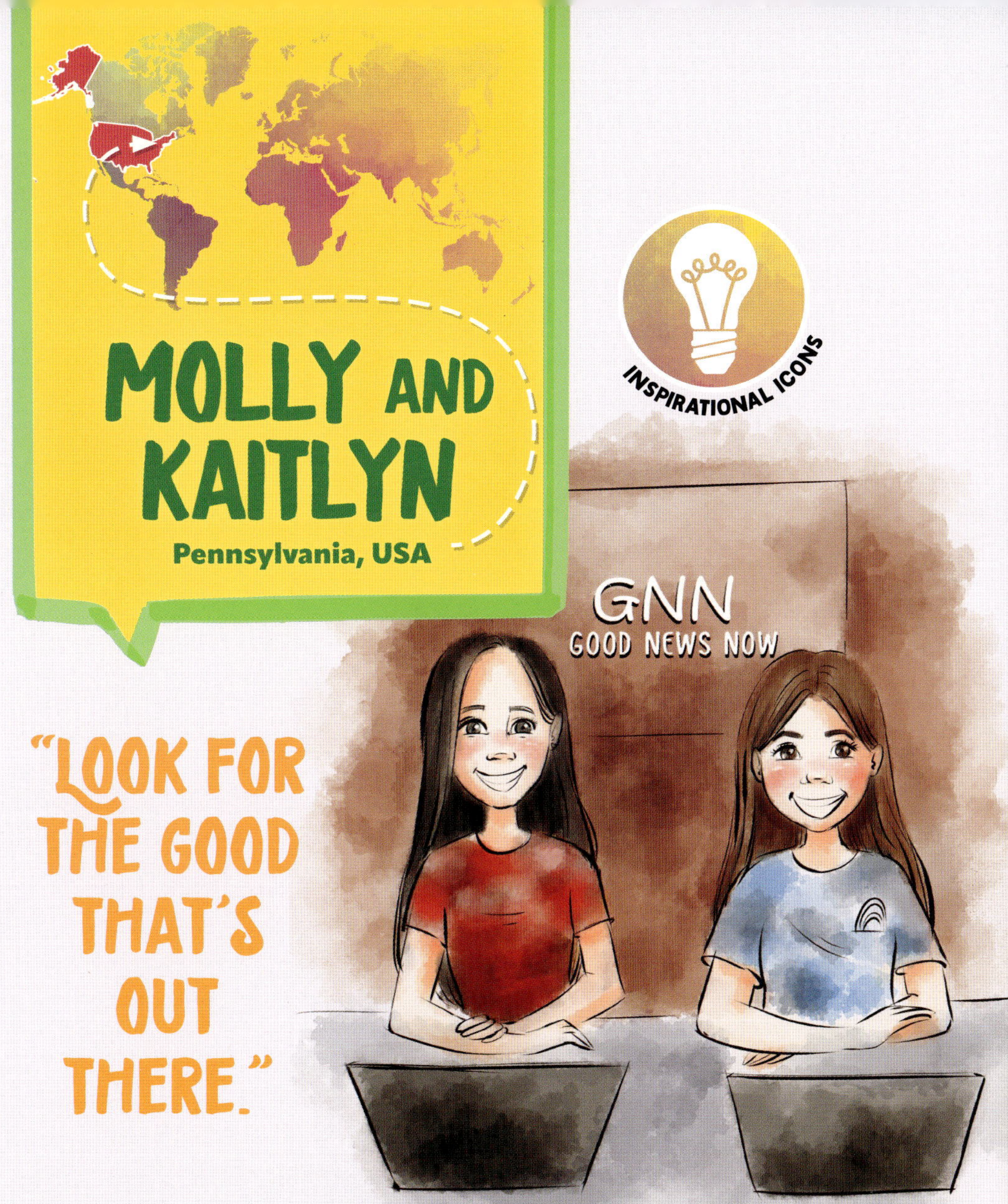

DO YOU EVER watch or read the news? Taking in too much negative news can make people tired, anxious, depressed, and it can even cause stomach problems.

Molly and Kaitlyn Harrington noticed people were feeling down because of everything going on in the world, specifically during the COVID-19 pandemic, and wanted to do something to raise people's spirits. They learned that hearing inspiring things makes people happier. So, they decided to try to find and share uplifting stories with the world.

The sisters asked their dad to record their news broadcast and started seeking out positive news. They reported about people making face masks and bakeries delivering treats to hospital workers. They shared the video on social media. They planned on only doing it once or twice, but after seeing the positive reaction, it turned into a weekly broadcast—they called it ***Good News Now* (GNN)**. They kept reporting on positive news including rediscovered species thought to be extinct and people planting millions of trees.

Now, they have a segment called GNN Heartfelt Heroes, which features people in their community who are helping others. The stories include people who have cooked meals for Ukrainian refugees, fixed donated cars and given them to families in need, and given free haircuts to the homeless.

Another one of their segments is GNN Kind Kids, which features kids who are helping their communities. Some stories they have reported on include kids helping stray animals get adopted, children who are running marathons to raise money for veterans, and a girl who is building wheelchairs for disabled pets.

Their community helps them by sharing their broadcasts on social media, sharing positive news with them and encouraging them to keep the show going. People around the world have told Molly and Kaitlyn that they look forward to their weekly positive news show.

When the girls began their journey, they had some self-doubt. They weren't sure they could make a difference or if anyone would watch the show. Molly worked hard

BECOME A YOUNG CHANGEMAKERS INSPIRATIONAL ICON!

- Focus on the good in the world. Look for the people helping others.
- Be a helper.
- Share good news with others.

to get comfortable reading her script in front of the camera. It was a challenge getting the word out about their show and finding people to watch it, but as their journey continued, their self-confidence grew. They both plan on continuing to help people see the good in the world.

MOLLY'S ADVICE FOR YOU:

If you want to make a difference, just start with a small first step. Small steps make big differences.

KAITLYN'S ADVICE FOR YOU:

There is so much good in our communities that is often overlooked. Once you start doing good, others will join you.

Molly

Kaitlyn

KAITLYN'S FUN FACTS:

- Kaitlyn sings in four choral groups for both her school and church.
- She has earned the Girl Scout Gold, Silver, and Bronze Awards.
- She has performed in over twenty-five musical productions like *Cinderella* and *The Lion King*.
- She enjoys karate.

MOLLY'S FUN FACTS:

- Molly plays percussion for her school's concert and jazz bands.
- She has won several championships as a softball pitcher.
- She has acted in several musicals, including *Beauty and the Beast* and *Annie*.
- She plays volleyball.

QUESTIONS FOR DISCUSSION

What is the most common reason that these Young Changemakers began their projects?

Which character traits do you notice most often in the Young Changemakers?

How do these character traits help the Young Changemakers work on their projects?

Do you see any of these character traits in yourself? Which ones? What are you doing when you see them?

What are the most common challenges and obstacles the Young Changemakers faced in carrying out their projects?

What people in your life would you ask for help if you started a project?

What is the most common need that the projects of the Young Changemakers support?

What need do you see in your community that could be supported by a Young Changemaker?